I Asked the Animals

Written by Eric C. Corsten
Illustrated by Rayah Jaymes

Copyright 2013
Published by Eric DaGoose Publishing

Dedication

To my only son, Ray Charles Corsten
My first wish is that you find the greatest
gift I could give you -- Creativity.
My second wish is that you use it wisely
I love you son...
Your Father

Eric Charles Corsten

I asked the turtle,
"Why are you so slow?"

He said,
"I have nowhere to go..."

"My feet are tired: this shell is heavy and hangs low."

"Besides..."

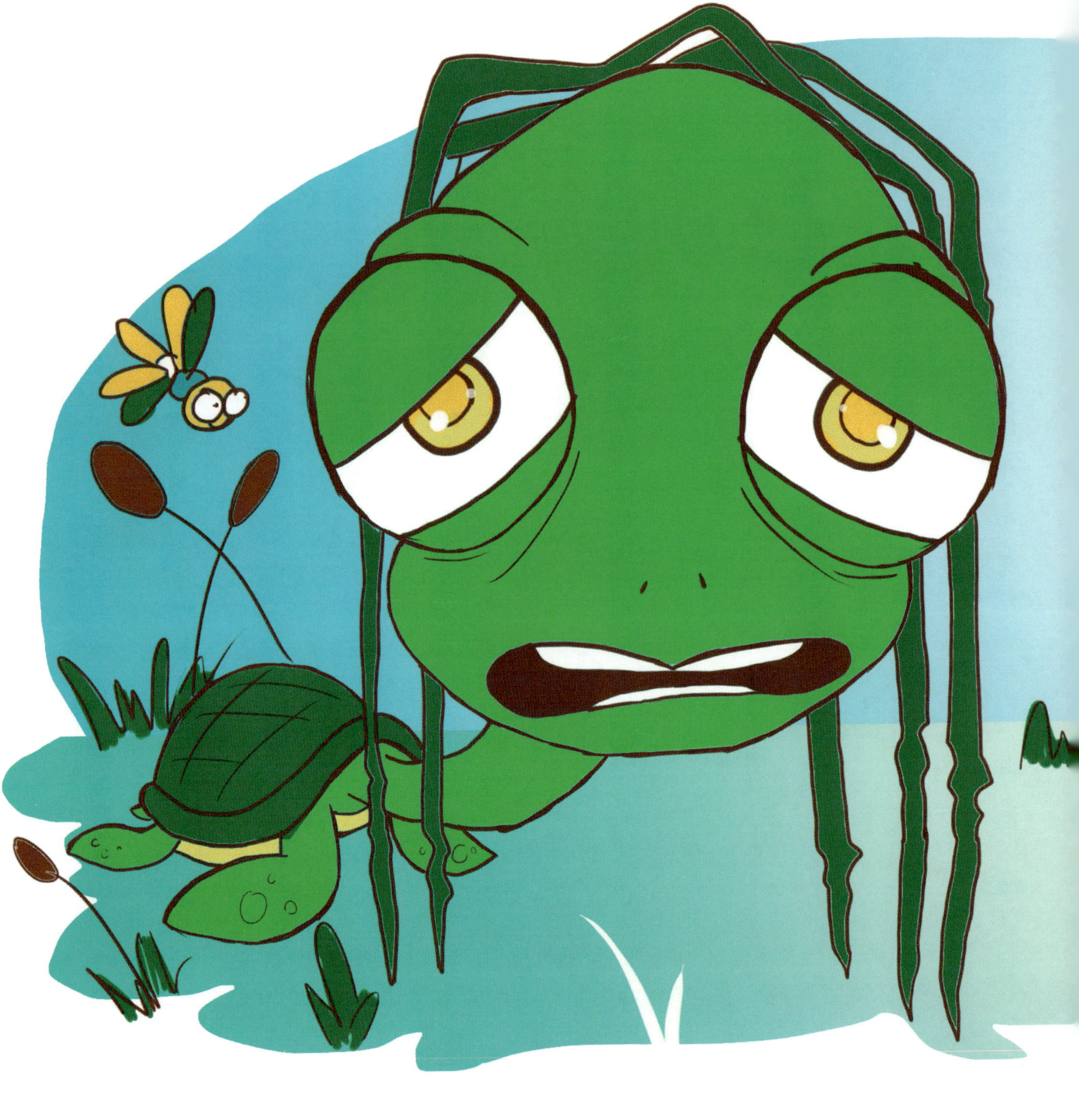

"Who wants to know?"

I asked the crow,
"Why do you sit on that wire?"

He said, "It's better than on a hot tire

Or wasting time trying to fly higher."

"By the way..."

"I'm selling this hay..."

"Do you have a buyer?"

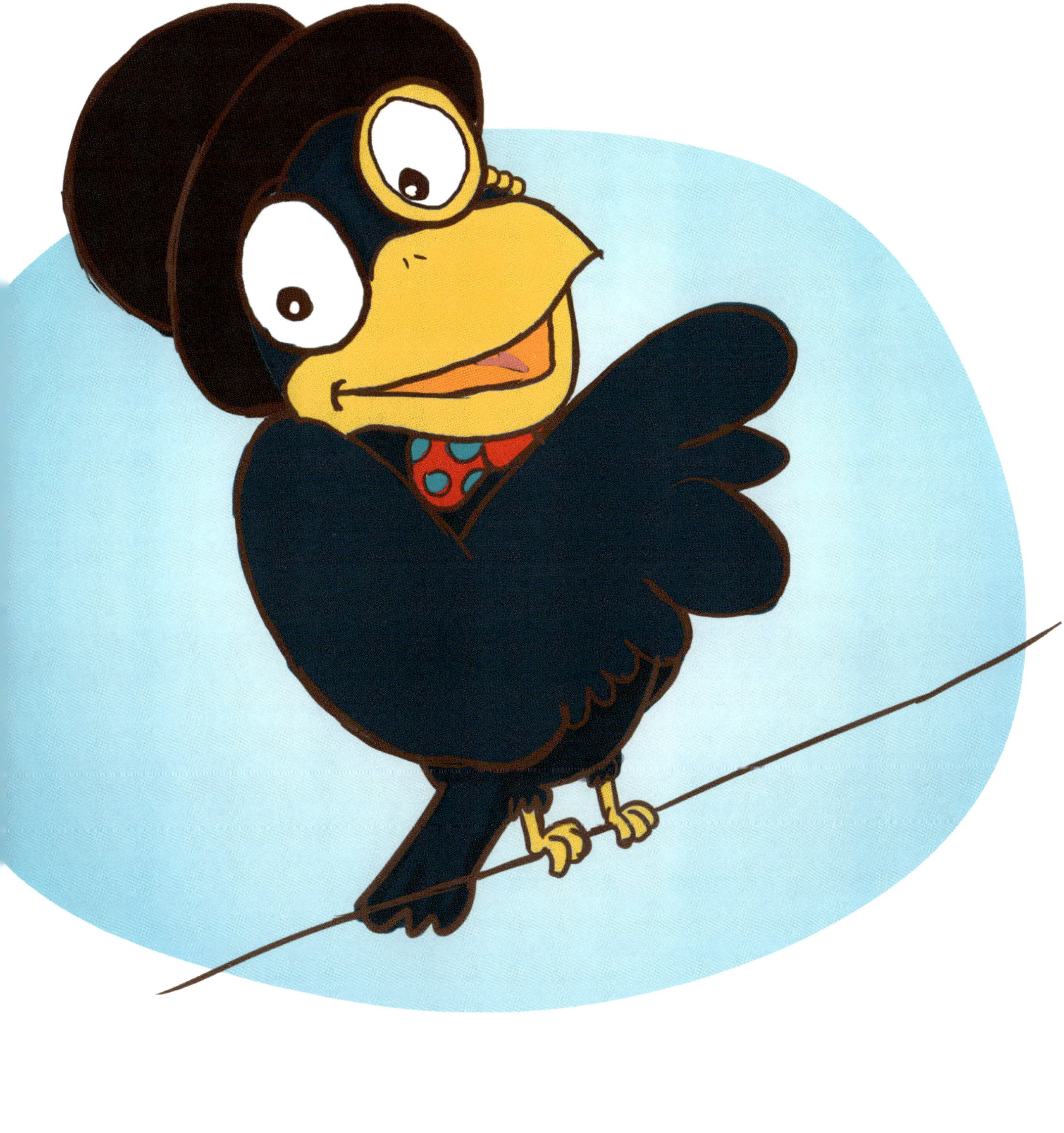

I asked the shire, "Why are you so fat?"

She said "I like to eat, what's wrong with that?"

"Would you like to come here and try on my hat?"

"This is all true, my shoes are bright blue"

"And you..."

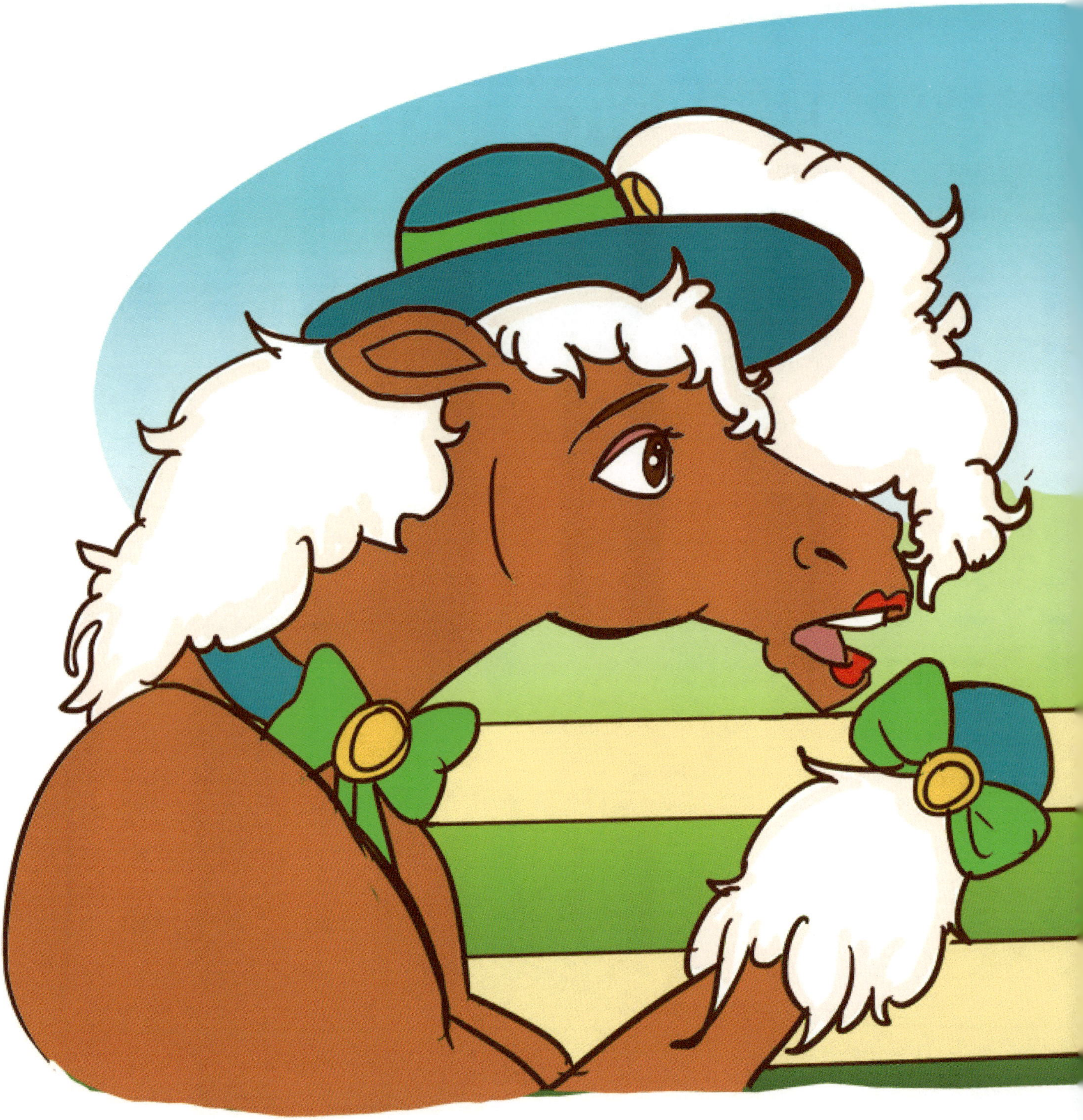

"Are a bit of a brat!"

I asked the cat,
"Why do you climb that tree?"

He said,
"You see that dog looking at me?"

"I don't think he wants crackers and brie."

"He thinks it's fun to run run run!

And to that..."

"I disagree."

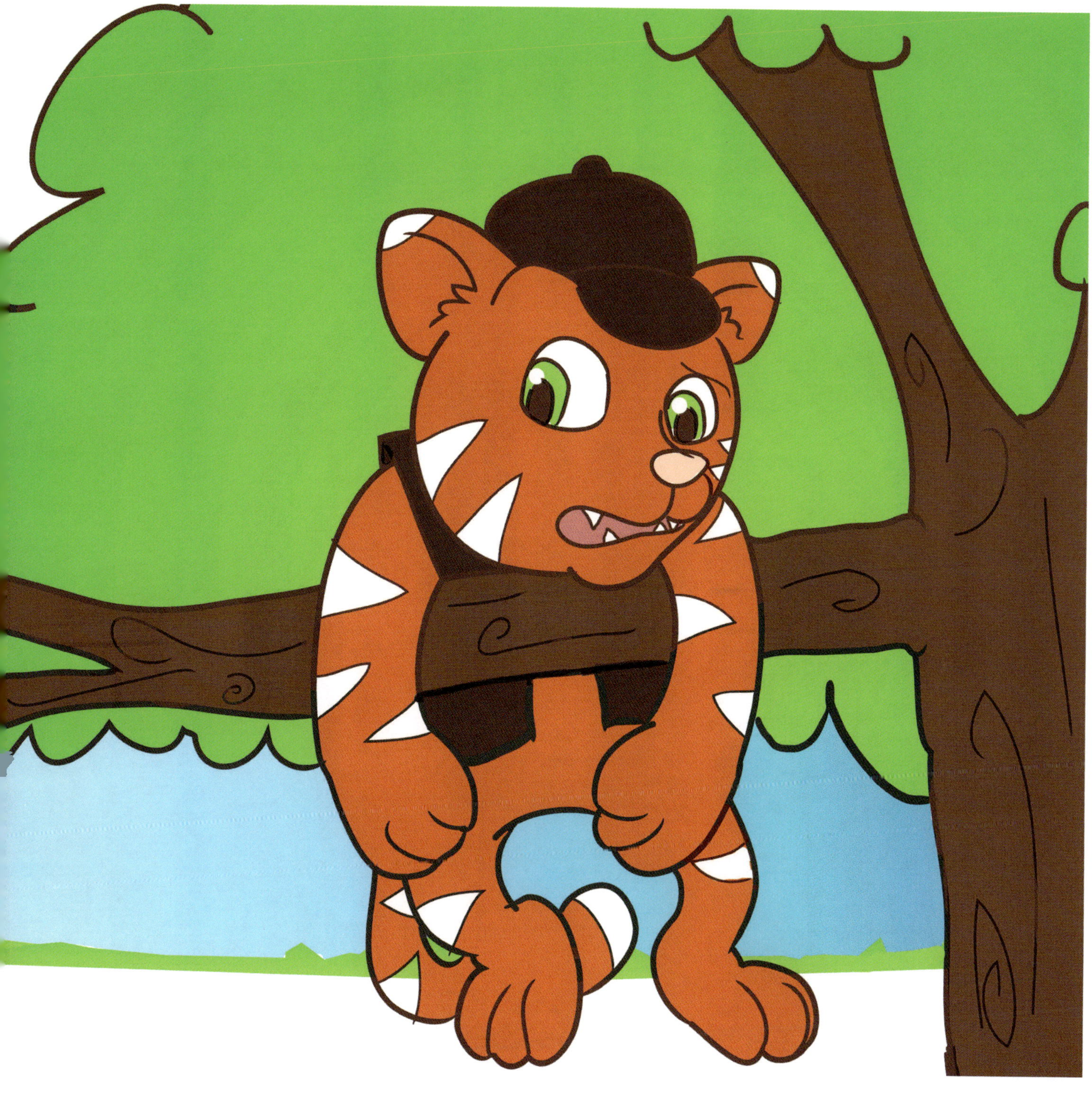

I asked the flea,
"Why do you munch on that sprig?"

He said, "Figs are too **BIG!**"

"Twigs are my gig."

"Please excuse me while I sleep in this pigs wig."

Just like that...

Into the feed I fell!

I shouted out
"Oh Well!"

split! splat! splat! split!

"How do you like that!?"

Made in the USA
Lexington, KY
08 August 2013